Was I Born This Way?
Or
"Late Diagnosis?"

I0160692

by

Jacqueline Francis

AB ASPECT Books
www.ASPECTBooks.com

———————————————

Copyright © 2019 Jacqueline Francis
Copyright © 2019 ASPECT Books, Inc.
ISBN-13: 978-1-4796-1108-9 (Paperback)
Library of Congress Control Number: 2019907459

Published by

AB ASPECT Books
www.ASPECTBooks.com

Table of Contents

Preface

Thank you, God, for the privilege of waking up! What a precious moment it is! I am not perfect. Romans 3:23 (NKJV) says, "For all have sinned and come short of the glory of God." I make mistakes, stumble, and fall, but you still give me that opportunity to keep learning and growing. There are times when I feel like giving up, when I don't have what it takes to complete the tasks before me. O Lord, let my eyes and my mind receive your Holy Spirit. You said you'll never leave me nor forsake me, so cover me with your precious blood.

Living with a disability is hard enough. But imagine going through life without knowing you are disabled. How can you learn to cope with a disability you do not know you have? How can you seek help if you do not know you need it? In this book, I will detail Sharon's struggles in living with a disability, discovering her disability and getting help. Sharon's life is full of misunderstandings and trials, some of which can be traced directly back to her disability. However, Sharon perseveres by believing in herself and trusting in God. God plays a big role in helping Sharon live her life with partial hearing loss and dyslexia. Like a friend once told her, "Your dreams should never be stopped by a disability. With determination and strength, you can accomplish your goals."

Introduction

My name is Sharon. It's my pleasure to invite you to delve into my book. It details my experiences with two different disabilities. I hope it can encourage you to overcome your circumstances and inspire you to fight for your dreams. I had to struggle through life with my disabilities and I still seek to achieve my dreams. But that has not stopped me. Keep reading and find out more

Chapter 1

No Red Flags

My name is Sharon. I was born in 1978, on the island of Jamaica, in the city of Kingston. The temperature in the middle of the year is a muggy heat at times, but a cool breeze would frequently visit from offshore. This is how it is in Kingston, Jamaica.

"Was I born this way?" I asked this question to myself so many times. When I was a child, I had no idea that I suffered from hearing loss. I am still not sure when it began. One may wonder if my parents ever recognized that I could not hear well. In my household, there was always someone available to carry messages, so it was not detected.

I recall playing a classroom game with my teacher and classmates when I was seven or eight years old and my teacher told one student something, who would then whisper it to another person, who would then whisper it to another student. It would continue to be whispered throughout the class until the last student heard the secret and revealed it to find out if that was what the teacher initially said. I was never successful at playing that game and now I know why.

Hearing loss was the reason to explain it. However, there was another reason. I watched a television show where two girls were friends, but the friendship went sour. One of the girls pretended to whisper something to the next girl in her ear and bit a piece of her ear off. After watching this TV show, I tried to avoid anyone who would want to whisper in my ear.

Mrs. Palmer, my 6th grade science teacher, was soft-spoken. From time to time, I could not hear what Mrs. Palmer said, and she was not the only one. However, when anyone put up their hand and asked her to repeat what she said, Mrs. Palmer would say, "Stop the talking and you will hear!" No one would be talking but she would always tell the class to stop talking. So even though I could not hear Mrs.

Palmer, I still did not take it as a sign that something may be wrong with my hearing.

Mrs. Palmer was a strict teacher. When she gave homework and the assignment was not completed in a way that was acceptable to her, she would make the non-compliant student feel less than himself or herself. She would call the student up to the front of the classroom and call him/her names like "dunce" and "good-for-nothing". Some children would go home and tell their parents. At the time, I was living with my father and I would not complain to him about a teacher. So, I would rudely talk back to Mrs. Palmer. For example, Mrs. Palmer would tell her students to bring peas and jam jars to school. She would put the peas in the jam jar and let them stay there to grow. Because I did not always bring in a jam-jar to school and would get in trouble for this, I would call Mrs. Palmer "peas' grains and jam jar."

I was known for misbehaving as a student in school. I played hooky, refused to turn in assignments, back-talked, and participated in many other activities of delinquency. At the root of many of these behaviors was the fact that I was not learning like everyone else in the class. As a student at that time, you were either smart or a dunce and I believed that I was a dunce and was categorized by teachers and fellow students alike as a dunce.

Ms. Williams, a teacher who used to reprimand me, became my mentor. Even though I was rude to Ms. Williams, this teacher was still interested in helping me. Ms. Williams showed me love and I responded gratefully to her intervention. I tried my best to be polite to Ms. Williams. I flourished under my mentor's encouragement. Ms. Williams tutored me on the weekends at her house. We worked hard together catching up on work and assignments that I missed or did not comprehend. Even though the time came for me to move up to seventh grade and Ms. Williams would not be my teacher anymore, she still continued our weekend tutoring sessions.

While it seems as if Ms. Williams was the only teacher who was mindful that I was not doing well academically because of her constant efforts to assist me, that is not the case. All of my teachers knew. But I was very rude and misbehaved quite a bit. Not many teachers would willingly assist a student who was rude, spiteful and disobedient. Ms. Williams was the only teacher who helped me even after I disrespected her and I never had to share my personal life.

I was a very rebellious child and much of my behavior was because I came from a broken home. As an adult, I can look back and confirm this rebellious behavior. But even in adulthood, I did not recognize that I might have hearing loss and that might have been the cause behind some of my rebellion. When my first child, a daughter, was about eighteen to twenty months, she would pull me to the window and point to the gate to get my attention. I was baffled at first, but when I looked out at the gate, I would see that someone was calling. Still, that did not send up a red flag. I would always say to myself, "This child of mine likes to look outside." But I never thought to myself that I was unable to hear what my child was hearing.

It seemed as if there were many ways for me to cope with hearing loss when I was both a child and adult. For example, there were many family members living in the same home together at the time that I had my first born, so, if I was called and did not hear that call, someone would come and tell me that I was being called. I continued to live with hearing loss, fully unaware of the problem. No one at work, school or home ever asked, "Do you hear well?" Or I never heard them ask.

During the 1990s, I made several trips to the United States from Jamaica for vacation. I remember in 1994 on one of my trips I stayed with my sister. My sister's boss went on vacation and brought back a phone for her. It was a unique phone. I never saw a phone like that before. It was small and had three colors of lights on it. Red, green, and blue. The red light would indicate that there was a message. The green light would let you know that the phone is ringing, and the blue light shows that a voicemail was left by a caller.

One day a friend of mine came over and the phone was ringing. My friend said out loud, "I never heard a phone that rings like a bird." I had never heard that phone ring because I would always look for the green light on the phone to see if someone was calling. "Pretty phone gives unique sound," was my response. Still no red flags. It was usually another phone in the house that notified me of an incoming call because its ring was much louder. I did not consider that I could not hear the unique sound of the pretty phone.

When my second child was about fifteen to nineteen months, she used to hold her ears, cry and call me to the kitchen. There were times when the glass kettle would be whistling, indicating that the water in it was boiling, but it did not dawn on me that I could not hear the whistle. My child had to pull me to the kettle so that I could hear it whistling. And every time she heard the whistle, my child started crying. When my husband came home, I told him that something was wrong with the child and described the experience to him. So, he put the kettle on the stove to boil in order to see what was wrong. As the kettle started boiling, our daughter ran to the kitchen door, covered her ears and called her dad. He still wanted to make sure everything was okay with the child. So, we decided to take the child to the doctor. The doctor had the child's ears tested and everything was normal.

After the doctor's appointment revealed that my child's auditory system was normal, I realized that I was the one with the hearing problem. I pointed one finger at my child, not realizing that more fingers were pointing back at me. This eye-opening moment changed my life forever. I decided to go to the ear doctor and to my amazement, discovered that I suffered from hearing loss.

Chapter 2

Finding Out

I was living a normal life not considering that I had any hearing loss and then the doctor tells me I have hearing loss. But more changes were coming and they came sooner than I thought. In New York, I started going to school for my High School Equivalency Diploma (G.E.D.). It was such a struggle for me and the frustration caused me to repeatedly stop taking the classes several times. However, it was my husband, Jonathan, who encouraged and also helped me to attain my G.E.D. He would do English, Math and Science drills with me many days of the week. It was not an easy road.

After getting my GED in 1996, I wanted to register for college. One of my GED teachers advised me to take a disability test. I found out that I had a learning disability. I was so shocked when I got the news. So shocked, that I got discouraged and stopped taking classes. I later took the disability test again in order to discern if the first test was valid. The results were the same. I brought the report home, showed my husband and we had a long talk about it. My husband tried to make me feel better about it. He would say, "You are not taking your time. You want to get it all in at once." So, I started doing one class at a time, but it was so hard. I gave up, again.

I decided to give school another try and resumed two years later. I always worked three or four times harder than other students. Even though my husband helped me, I would make a lot of mistakes. I would replace 'm' with 'w', 'l' for the number 7, and 's' for 5. For words such as 'and', I would write 'dna'. For the word 'have', I would write 'of'. Instead of writing, 'no' I would write 'on'. The list of mistakes I would make was endless. When my husband would see those mistakes, he would tell me "Take your time! You are not thinking straight, Sharon."

One teacher realized that I may have a disability, and decided to sit with me to examine what was going on. After writing an essay and turning it in to my teacher, the teacher noticed that my name was spelt backwards. The teacher's suspicion was confirmed and he advised me to go to a place where I could go and get some tests done for myself. I went to the facility and completed the tests and the results were the same as the other two that I had done before. Now I had three tests with the same results from three different places. I made sure not to inform those who administered the tests the second and third times that I was tested before. I asked all three doctors the same question, "How does someone get dyslexia?" They replied that it could be a family history, or it can develop on its own. I responded, "Do you think this is a genetic disorder?" The doctor would say, "I don't know. It is a possibility, but not always."

When I found out that I was dyslexic, I was so sad, but a little relieved to know that there is help and hope for me to learn. I can now look back and say that I am glad I never gave up. With God, all things are possible. I accepted the disorder, and decided that if I am going to be successful in school, I would have to work harder.

I struggled with my disability for many, many, years. As a child in school, I made reading errors and complained about my reading difficulties. I had strong reasoning and thinking skills, even though I was a slow reader. Most of the time, my sentence structure was not correct. Many subjects and verbs did not agree. I only realized these mistakes after the teacher's correction of my school work. I struggled with understanding parts of a sentence. When my teachers called on me to go in front of the class to read, the teacher would find that I had disappeared. I had trouble reading unfamiliar words, often making wild guesses because I could not sound out the word. I had trouble remembering dates, names, and telephone numbers. I produced messy handwritten assignments that were difficult to read and demonstrated poor spelling skills. I struggled to finish my tests on time, and it was rare for me to turn in a completed test. Even now as an adult, I have many of the same problems in school. I used to get so discouraged and as a result, I did not want to continue in school.

When I was first diagnosed with my learning disability, I was so embarrassed and ashamed. I kept starting and stopping classes. It was like riding a roller coaster that goes up and down. My husband always gave me support, so I went back and worked harder. When it was time for me to take the exam for my class, I became very nervous and anxious. I failed by ten points, so I stopped going to school again. My husband and children encouraged me to go back.

I went back with full confidence the next time. It was not easy but, I give God thanks for the help I got. I got extended time for tests and exams, separate locations for test-taking, directions read and re-read aloud, and use of a calculator. Also, I was provided with extended time for in-class assignments and tests, a printed summary of class material and a breakdown of large assignments into several small tasks. I was so happy for the help which led to success. So, I gave my best effort to my school work and was able to achieve my academic goal.

When you accomplish one dream, like going to college and successfully completing your coursework, then great joy will come. You can rejoice over your accomplishments. Now, I can tell others who have the same problem not to be ashamed. Go and get help.

The only thing I wish I could do now is just study and do my exams without help, just like my husband and children. I am still happy for my achievement. It's a good feeling to sit down in a college class and achieve my goals.

I am no longer ashamed of my struggle with dyslexia and have accepted it. It means I have to work more carefully and review my written assignments carefully. I also realized that I was not alone and that there are many people who have the same problem as me and are doing well in school.

I realize that sometimes when you are around people who are educated and they know that you are not, they like to look down on you or make you feel less than yourself. If you give into those feelings, you will have low self-esteem. Never, ever put yourself down that way. You can get your education if you want, but you must try, try and try. Happy days will come if you stick it out and go to school. You will have ups and downs but you must push yourself if you want that dream. Don't just dream the dream and believe that the dream will be realized without effort.

Today, I give God thanks for my children. They didn't have to go through the struggle I went through growing up in school. They are very smart kids. They excelled in their classes and made the honor roll.

Looking back at my life now, I can see where my attitude and behavior played a great role in causing people to withdraw from me. I did not know how to handle coming from a broken family. And to top it off, I had hearing loss and dyslexia. I regret not knowing about these problems when I was younger. I am still proud that I was able to get help and achieve a part of my dreams and goals. Knowing the cause of my problems might have made the help I needed available and I would be further along the path to academic success.

Growing up in the Caribbean with a learning disability was challenging. Teachers did not know about disability issues when I was going to school in the 1980s. Some teachers made learning more difficult for such children. They would call them all kinds of names like "stupid" and "idiot." They did not motivate these students to learn. Instead they made them feel like failures. That's how I felt - like a total failure. The teachers made me feel bad, and by not having my parents there to stand by my side, I began to believe I was alone. While many teachers were not on my side, I had this one teacher that did not want to give up on me. This one teacher saw the potential in me and helped me in whatever way she could. This teacher was one of the reasons why I never gave up on myself and my dreams.

We do not choose our disability. Disability chooses us. Because of my situation, I never look down on someone who doesn't have education, or doesn't receive the help they need. I would always lend my hand to those who are seeking help to further their education. People with a learning disability should never stop following their goals and dreams. They should be motivated to strive for what they want.

Living in America provides you with many new opportunities. There are schools that are free, so you don't have to pay for education. There are public libraries you can go to for information and help in obtaining a High School Equivalency Diploma. There are public schools that offer night school to adults. After obtaining your GED, one should not stop there. Individuals should encourage themselves to go on to college. When going to college, there is financial aid and payment plans available, and you can take classes at your own pace. They offer special assistance for those with learning disabilities such as extra help in class and more time for testing. Some people with learning disabilities are not aware that there are many opportunities available to help them fulfill their dreams of getting an education. Hiding your disability is a disadvantage. When you open up to the right people, you can get help. I learned this after struggling for years of not knowing there were others like me who are getting the help they need.

"Lord, I believe you have a special plan for my life. Whatever that purpose is, may You help me to do it earnestly, in your name, Jesus. Lord, thank You for giving me a wonderful and caring family, and loyal trustworthy friends who encourage me in the Lord always. In Christ is everlasting strength."

When I open my eyes and look at the beautiful day -- the sun, the moon and the stars, I see the power of God. It is a new day. I appreciate the journey I am on. Father God, victory is on the way. I choose to keep praying and have faith no matter what comes".

Chapter 3

Thanks to God

I struggled with loneliness when I was young. I was often irritated with everyone and everything. I had lots of reasons to feel that way. Coming from a broken family, I didn't know how to reach out. The only thing I knew was bitterness and anger. I did not know Jesus and had no one to embrace me. My loneliness took a long time to overcome. Now, I am older and I am getting to know Jesus better every day. Even though I know a little about Jesus, I still have bad days when I feel burdened. Thank God I have His amazing love. The more time I spend with Jesus is the more I develop a better relationship with Him. Sometimes when crisis comes at me or my children, I become so anxious. Like most Christians, I sometimes forget to cry out to my Heavenly Father when the burdens of life seem too heavy to bear and then I remember that He never leaves me nor forsakes me. I tell myself that the negativity and accusation will come, but what matters is how I handle the situation in God's sight. Whatever I do, it should look good to God for His perfect example.

I thank God for this country and my husband. I know that if I was still in the Caribbean, I would not have accomplished what I have. I still have that fear when I am suddenly called to read or speak publicly. I get very nervous and anxious. Looking at me, you could not tell that I am anxious and nervous. If I am asked to do something in advance, that works better for me because I can prepare myself for whatever I have to do.

I pray: "Father God, you are my Physician. I thank you for all the healing you grant to me. You know what I have been through in my life. You know how much I can handle when I get bad news from my doctor. May you continue taking care of me and my needs, giving me more faith, and peace. Help me to remember that life is not guaranteed. It is unpredictable so it's my duty to make the best of it each day. Speak with kindness, act with humility and have God present".

Some days, the journey of life looks bad. We must remember to take care of ourselves. Sometimes we can get too busy taking care of others and forget that we are important too. It makes me happy to be helpful. But you have others who only call when they need something. As soon as they get it, you don't hear from that individual again. So, it is important to focus on yourself at times. Your happiness is important.

Now, when people throw their negative words at you, know that they are not seeing the good light in you. Try not to stoop down to their level but throw some love with kind words to them and hope they catch on to the words. These words of love may inspire them to change from their negative ways. There are people in the world that make people's lives miserable and difficult, because of mistakes. The known and the unknown mistakes. They criticize, judge and gossip about the mistake. They will try to ruin your life and your reputation. It's not so easy to love and trust your brothers and sisters. As soon as something goes wrong, they will start talking about you. Every one of us has skeletons in the closets and we may not share it with friends and family. We all should give God the praise because if He puts all our sins out for everyone to see, then maybe no one would want to be associated with us.

I thank God for my trials. Trials are blessings in the end. No matter how stormy life gets, I try not to let it get me down, but it does sometimes. I will always be thankful and try to smile. You will get disappointed when things happen outside your expectations. Try not to assume the worse. Pray more and try to smile more. I think of how blessed I am to have a family. That was one of my dreams and that makes me laugh often. The beauty in life is rising up when you fall.

Chapter 4

A Word of Encouragement

The past year has not been a good year for me. On the one hand, there is always bad news. I am struggling with school work and on days when I can't get it, I feel overwhelmed and I want to give up. I have been praying for relief. But it seems as if there is no end in sight. This is reflected in the daily prayers below.

Some days, the sadness is overbearing. On these days, I feel as if I am walking through life like the walking dead. It was on a day like this that I received a call from one of my nephews. We had not spoken to each other in a while. What is so significant about this call is that I was sitting at home feeling depressed and alone. The call came in from Caswell Blake and at that moment, I was wishing for someone to speak to me. Caswell had been living in a different location, and I had lost track of him. Without knowing what I was going through, he said to me,

"The sweetest moment in life comes not with the greetings you receive but with the thought that someone wishes the best for you every day. You are created by God so you should create your life as a garden. Plant kindness and compassion. Water with love and gratitude. Then, you will enjoy the beauty of your life. Remember we can't have all that we desire but time will give us all that we deserve." September 11, 2018, 10:50 AM

I hope that this thought will encourage others as it has encouraged me.

You need to remember that there are some people who will not be happy for you. They are only happy in front your face but behind your back is another thing. So, the one who is happy in your face and happy behind your back, is the one you need to keep close to you. You have to pray for the ones who are trying to hold you back and keep moving on. When happiness comes to you, you have to be so careful of who you share it with. All will not be happy for you.

"Praying is important. I have to ask the Lord to show me the people who are not there for me. People think when they are not happy for me, my happiness stops. No! No one can take my happiness from me but God. They may try and think it will work, but no, it will not. I am so happy because I have Christ in my heart."

"I cannot give love to those who don't want it, and I cannot change back the hands of times with all the right answers for all the wrongs. I enjoy my life journey with my husband, children, and all those who appreciate me. I don't look at what I have in my life but who I have in my life. Every day is a journey. It comes with smiles, with tears and with discouragement. This is my journey, so I have to be happy when these

I never liked to explain myself to people who I know do not like me and want priority in my life when they do not deserve a place of priority.

things come my way. You have to show that you value yourself. If not, no one will do it for you."

Chapter 5

Final Thoughts to Parents

When you're a parent it is important to be there for your children and to watch them grow. When you abandon your children, it can leave a negative impact on their life, especially if the child has a learning disability. Without a parent's guidance, it could be very challenging for children growing up. When a child is not aware of their disability and not sure why they are not normal as others, this can cause them to have low self-esteem. Thank God that my self-esteem was not low in spite of my disability and lack of parental involvement. I still persevered toward my dream of gaining an education.

No matter what the disability is, children as well as adults can make progress one step as a time. For a child, when things don't seem to go the right way, there are professionals whom one may contact to seek help. These may include doctors, teachers, and other specialists for guidance. It may also be beneficial to seek support from groups within the community. It is a chance for parents to interact with each other and pinpoint strategies that may help them with their child/children.

Children should always have their parent's support. Even when children make wrong choices, parents should still stand by their side and try their best to guide them and not leave them on their own. Children still need to acknowledge their mistakes as their parents correct them, and try not to repeat the same ones. When we pray, we must pray for all the children, not just ours. Prayer is power.

Parents, try and spend time with your children and find out how they are doing in school. If a teacher says that they need extra help in school, make it happen for him or her or them, as the case may be. Find out what's going on in class. By doing this, you can find out about any red flags that indicate your child has a disability or learning disorder.

If they have any problems, you can proceed to getting them the kind of help they would need right away. If they have a learning disability, don't let them feel less than themselves. When you give up on your children, they can develop trust issues. As a parent, try to always guide your children on the right path, and to show them what is wrong and what is right. Give them all the help and support you have. Parents, if you alone cannot help your child, there are a lot of libraries that help children and adults and even the guidance counselors in the schools. Make use of the opportunity to help yourself and to help others as well.

Do not use words and phrases like "dunce", "not smart", "foolish", and "waste of time". Their self-esteem will go low, and it may take them a long time to overcome these words. I used to hear those words from teachers. They are hurtful words to use to a child or children. But words can't put you down unless you allow it to stay inside of you. At your lowest, weakest and darkest moments, God is your comforter.

This is why it is important for parents to be there for their child or children. It is also very important to make sure your child gets a good education, especially if the opportunity was not provided for the parent. Break the cycle and make sure your child is provided with the opportunity for education. There are so many programs in America that assist both adults and children in getting a good education.

Try not to compare your child or children to others or to a sibling. When a child is born, no one knows how that child will develop. A disability should not mean that a child or children should be mistreated. Parents, encourage your child or children to stay in school! But the traditional educational path may not be for our children. If you see and know that your children or child cannot manage the classwork of college, nothing is wrong with a trade. It is better to have a trade than to have nothing at all. If they don't want to go to college, let them develop a trade. Don't let them give up and feel sorry for themselves. A certification in a trade is as good as a degree.

When children become adults, parents must still be there for them, especially if the child has a specific disability. They may still need guidance. But there must be a balance between guidance and letting a child live their own adult life. Adults can make wrong choices and bad decisions. We must show them love. We have to let our children live their lives and make their own mistakes. It may seem difficult for you to let a disabled child, who is now an adult, live their own life. The adult has to be able to cope or at least learn how to cope with their disability on their own because you, the parent, will not always be there.

Adult children with disabilities may also have to deal with their own children who may disrespect them because of their disability. For example, if the parent with a disability is not able to get a professional career, they may have to settle for low paying jobs. Their child may be embarrassed by their parents' job and will respond to parents with disrespect because of their embarrassment. The parent is doing their best to provide for their family. The child should appreciate what their parents are doing for them and show love to their parents.

Chapter 6

Closing Words

Many people have hearing loss. It can be frustrating especially when trying to understand other people as they speak in a normal tone of voice. One may not want to acknowledge the fact of not hearing properly, and can give an answer not related to a question being asked. This is dangerous, especially in a court of law when being addressed by a judge or lawyer. Communication issues can also cause arguments within a family because a member or members have poor hearing. In another case, some people may have to repeat what they say because you think they are mumbling. Also, the television or radio volume may be turned up too high for others with normal hearing. There is help in the form of hearing aid or cochlear implants. But not everyone can get the implants or hearing aid.

It can be frustrating asking people to repeat themselves numerous times. It may seem better to remove yourself from the conversation altogether. Sometimes, you feel like you are being ignored when you ask someone to repeat yourself and at that point, you can get offended and display a bad attitude. On occasion, when someone repeats what they said loudly, it may be interpreted as a bad attitude and you may respond in kind, which may start an argument.

Interacting with people is a process, especially when you have hearing loss. Walking away from a conflict is a good way to deal with these issues, but walking away does not solve the problem. It may help to continue with the confrontation and get everything out. Misinterpretations may be clarified and honesty can provide a gateway for open communication. It can help to have someone mediate the situation to make sure voices are not too loud and the intent of both sides of the conflict is understood. It is possible to interact with the world if you suffer from hearing loss. It just takes some effort.

Dyslexia, although it may me a setback for many people, it can have some strengths. Being dyslexic can help someone excel. For example, excellent puzzle solving skills, brilliant reasoning, great conversationalists, and a good memory for stories are some of the successes that people with dyslexia have achieved. Research has concluded that few can keep track of the characters and plot twists and turns in a story better than some dyslexics. Personally, I have found that I am able to present solutions to problems presented to me. I am good at reasoning through an issue. But dyslexia also has its downsides.

God created each and every one of us in a unique way. He knows all the details of our lives. The promise of the Lord is the blessing for those who trust in Him and pray and bring supplication to him.

School work seems to easier for everyone else around me. But not me. It takes a lot of effort for me to complete what some would say is a simple task. If in conversation, someone says a word I do not understand, I cannot respond immediately. I have to look up the definition and then respond. I have noticed that I have to go through this process often. I have to read a passage more than one time to comprehend what is being said. Patience and time is needed in order for me to truly, fully, completely understand what I am reading. Reading anything short is good because it is easier to comprehend. Taking notes also helps me to remember the important details. It may seems difficult to live with dyslexia when you think that you alone have that problem. When you are enlightened and you know that so many different people have that problem, it becomes more acceptable to you. Also having the support from your family makes you feel amazing.

As most of us already know, parenting is very challenging. At some point in life, children will defy the wishes of their parents. It may be occasional or becomes a pattern of the child/ children for a variety of reasons. A child may respond with disobedience and disrespect if a parent loses his/ her temper. By contrast, the child becomes more obedient when you remain calm and "cool". The child will gain respect when you respect him or her, and other members of the family. Children learn what they see. Now, when a child is obedient and respectful, complement him/ her and even give a reward. This will also help to build self-esteem. We must keep a watchful eye on our children, as well as the company they keep. Bad company may influence and encourage your obedient and respectful child to do something unlawful. It is wise to even check their room occasionally, and make it our duty to ask questions when situations seem abnormal.

It is important to listen to teachers because they know the signs of a learning disability and they interact with you child/children for many hours of the day. When children know that they are not comprehending like others, they tend to withdraw from the learning process and lack the desire to participate in class. Teachers will be aware of this behavior and can inform parents of things that can be done to remedy the problem.

Sometimes a child will misbehave and be mischievous in order to draw attention to themselves. They may need attention and not know how to express themselves in a way that will not be embarrassing to them, especially if the teacher is stern, strict or serious. They would not want to approach them. So misbehavior maybe a clue to a deeper problem.

It's very important to monitor your child. When they come home from school make sure they are doing their homework. If they constantly say they do not have homework, that's a red flag. The student may not understand their homework or may not know how to tell you that they do not understand. So follow up with the teachers and inspect your child's school book. Show interest in your child. Find out if they are getting homework. If they are getting homework, let them get the help they need. It is better to be helped when you are younger as opposed to when you are an adult.

I did not find out about my disabilities until I was an adult and I felt very embarrassed and ashamed. I was happy when my husband could embrace the situation. He made me feel more confident in myself. We have so much more knowledge about hearing loss, dyslexia and how to live with disability now. Why not avail yourself of the help that can be provided? Do not suffer in silence. Let someone who you can trust know what's wrong. There is always help for you.

Crying Out to God

Daily Devotions

Day 1

I give God thanks for this day. I am at home and it is a troublesome day for me, but I won't give up. I know people are crazy and sad, so dear Lord, please bless me with nothing apart from happiness as I go through the day. Grant these troubled ones' peace of mind where they will find love. When I pray and in my walking with you Lord, I feel the joy and happiness you want for me inside. Psalms 34:8 KJV O taste and see that the Lord is good: blessed is the man that trusteth in him.

Day 2

Good morning God! I have to believe that You are going to make something wonderful happen, even with all the ups and down I am having. Amen. I am leaving the stress at work and going home to relax. I will not allow people to block my blessing. I put my trust in You, Father God. I know You will not disappoint me Lord. Isaiah 4 KJV Trust ye in the Lord forever: for in the lord Jehovah is everlasting strength

Day 3

Dear God, If I could only talk to these people who call themselves Christians, these would be my words to them: make a difference with a good word that touches the heart and love more to inspire the person who is doing those bad things and give encouragement. 2Thessalonians 3:5 KJV And the Lord direct your hearts into the love of God, and into the patient waiting for Christ.

Day 4

Dear God, I don't have a peaceful mind and a joyful heart. Help me to keep a smile on my face and remove all of the doubts I am feeling. I will still have a blessed day. God keep me in good health, bless my family and multiply my finances so that I can help some of those people who need help. Take away my pains and my worries, dear Lord. Proverbs 17:22 KJV. A merry heart doeth good like a medicine: but a broken spirit drieth the bones.

Day 5

Everything happens for a reason but Lord, I don't know the reason. I need your help. How long will this last? I know You will never leave me or forsake me, even when I feel alone. I feel like I am going through a dark tunnel but I have to trust God no matter how dark the situation is. God is who I put my trust in. Romans 12:12 KJV Rejoicing in hope; patient in tribulation; continuing instant in prayer.

Day 6

In the name of the Lord, I have to succeed regardless of negative people. Be fair with me and my family. Thank you, God, for waking me up today. Please give me wisdom, patience and faith. Lord I am relying on your promises and your goodness in your words. Psalms 46:1KJV God is our refuge and strength, a very present help in trouble.

Day 7

It's the Sabbath day. I have more peace of mind. I don't have to worry about the things of the world. Thank You, Lord, for the Sabbath. It's a beautiful, sun-shining day. Life comes with problems, but we have a loving God who is protecting and helping in His time. Psalms 27: 14 KJV Wait on the lord: be of good courage, and he shall strengthen thine heart; wait, I say on the lord.

Day 8

A word from a friend: You have many reasons to say thank you God. It's going to be ok. Proverbs 10:17 KJV He is in the way of life that keepeth instruction: but he that refuseth reproof erreth.

Day 9

Thank you, Lord! Dear Jesus, my experience today is not a good one. May Your will be done in Your name, Father God! Amen. Help me to rejoice in You Lord. Psalms 55:22 KJV. Cast thy burden upon the lord, and he shall sustain thee: he shall never suffer the righteous to be moved.

Day 10

The mistakes I make, place them under my feet and use them to raise me up, not to let the weight crush me down. With the love of our Father, there is no limit and his power comes with all strength. Mark 11:24 KJV Therefore I say unto you, whatsoever things ye desire, when ye pray, believe that ye receive them, and ye shall have them.

Day 11

Thank you, Lord, for another day. I pray that this day will be a productive day for me. Bless my going out and my coming in, in Jesus name. Lord because of your compassion to me I will always be faithful to you. 1Peter 4:16 KJV Yet if any man suffer as a Christian, let him not be ashamed, but let him glorify God on this behalf.

Day 12

Father God, help me to see the good in these people who have done bad things to me and my family. Help me to keep my faith in you. Thank you for your blessing, strength, comfort and peace all day. Amen. Romans 12:21 KJV. Be not overcome of evil, but overcome evil with good.

Day 13

Today, I give you thanks for my family. Nothing is impossible when I ask God to work out things on our side. Keep us safe, strong and courageous in all that comes our way. I give you all the glory and thanks in advance. Amen Jeremiah33:3 KJV Call unto me, and I will answer thee, and shew thee great and mighty things, which thou knowest not.

Day 14

When I pray, it helps me to let go of a bad habit. I pray no matter what comes my way, even though it is hard to do sometimes. In life, I must have faith and live by faith, with patience and understanding. I am grateful that you woke me up this morning to sing praises to your name Lord. Psalm 37:4 KJV Delight thyself also in the lord, and he shall give thee the desires of thine heart.

Day 15

Lord, help me make this day a better day than yesterday. Please supply my needs and keep blessing me with the opportunities I need. Amen. I will not let these people take away your blessing from me. I will fight my battles with prayer and I know the Lord will answer me. Psalms 91:2 KJV I will say of the lord, he is my refuge and my fortress: My God; in him will I trust

Day 16

Faith makes everything possible. Hope makes everything work. Love is beautiful so I must keep everything positive with God's love. 1 Corinthians 13:13 KJV. And now abideth faith, hope, charity, these three; but the greatest of these *is* charity.

Day 17

Father God, my promises are to trust you and your words and to make a difference for someone, by encouragement or inspiration, with a pure heart that has no secret motive. Give me courage when I am scared and directions when I feel like I am going to lose my walk with you. Help me to always be focused on you God, in Jesus name I pray, Amen. Proverbs 5:21 KJV For the ways of man are before the eye of the lord, and he pondereth all his goings.

Day 18

Lord, it's another day. Help me to embrace the bad news if it comes my way. People will be people. Help me to handle this problem, Lord. Let them know that they are loved so they don't need to do bad things to people. John 16:33 KJV. These things I have spoken unto you, that in me ye might have peace. In the world ye shall have tribulation: but be of good cheer; I have overcome the world.

Day 19

Father, I humbly come to You. Take away fear from me, and give me some peace and joy. I need it, oh Lord. Amen. Keep out those who are doing harm to me and my family, Lord. Help them to make good, Godly decisions, Lord. Proverbs 4:23 KJV

Keep thy heart with all diligence; for out it are the issues of life.

Day 20

Today, I don't feel happy, loved, or strong, Lord. Please protect me and bless me with your love. Guide me with your comfort. Dear God, today I want to lift up my family, I ask that you will protect us Lord. Keep us out of danger and give us the strength at this time Lord. We need you Lord. Help us to lean on you more, Father God. Psalms 27:1 KJV. The Lord is my light and my salvation; who shall I fear; the lord is the strength of my life; of who shall I be afraid.

Day 21

Happy day! It is the Sabbath. Lord help me to make it in the heavenly kingdom, Lord. What a day that will be. I hope to see it all. Romans 15: 13 KJV Now the God of hope fill you with all joy and peace in believing, that ye may abound in hope, through the power of the Holy Ghost

Day 22

Give me the strength today, Oh Lord. Amen. Dear God, it has been a long time since I have had a relaxed mind and a happy spirit with a good soul.

Give me a heart full of love so I can love these people, Lord. Amen. There is nothing beautiful like God's love. His love is healthy and beautiful. Galatians 5:22,23 KJV But the fruit of the Spirit is love, joy, peace, longsuffering, gentleness, goodness, faith, Meekness, temperance: against such there is no law.

Day 23

It's a beautiful day, Oh Lord. Help me with a miracle. Take away the pain and show me a way to smile. Father, take my worries and fears. I know the problem will be solved but I need to know how. My heart is full of fears. Jeremiah 29:13 KJV. And ye shall seek me, and find me, when ye shall search for me with all your heart

Day 24

Lord, I need to have a peace of mind with You. Help me though out the rest of the day. Grant me this experience with you. Make this day a good one, Lord. I don't know what will be thrown at my family, but I have to be strong and remember that you can break those who think they are stronger than you. Zephaniah 3:17 KJV The Lord thy God in the midst of thee is mighty; he will save, he will rejoice over thee with joy; he will rest in his love, he will joy over thee with singing.

Day 25

Today, I place my family in your care God. Lord, I need you to lead me to use the right words today. Lord, help me to make these decisions I need to make. I need you to send the Holy Spirit to give me the direction needed for this situation, Lord, please, Father God. **James 1:5 KJV.** If any of you lack wisdom, let him ask of God, that giveth to all men liberally, and upbraideth not; and it shall be given him.

Day 26

Oh Lord, I pray to you because I still don't have that happy inner feeling. Let my day be light so that I can smile and pray for those who are making things so bad. **Ezekiel 36:26** KJV A new heart also will I give you, and a new spirit will I put within you: and I will take away the stony heart out of your flesh, and I will give you a heart of flesh.

Day 27

Father God, today I am not going to make fear or other negative things take away the joy of a good day. I believe in you and I believe in myself too. **Psalm 19:14** KJV Let the words of my mouth, and the meditation of my heart, be acceptable in thy sight, O LORD, my strength, and my redeemer.

Day 28

Today is your day Lord. It is the Sabbath day, so I will meditate on you. You are the God of the valley and the mountain, so I give you thanks for the good and the bad times. **Psalm 77:11-12** KJV I will remember the works of the LORD: surely I will remember thy wonders of old. [12]I will meditate also of all thy work, and talk of thy doings.

Day 29

Thank you, Father God. Today's life is for doing what is good. There are opportunities today. Leave yesterday's mistakes and have hope for today. Live it, love it; it's your day. The Lord gives it to you. Psalm 51:1-2 KJV Have mercy upon me, O God, according to thy lovingkindness: according unto the multitude of thy tender mercies blot out my transgressions. Wash me thoroughly from mine iniquity, and cleanse me from my sin.

Day 30

Good morning, Lord. I feel like I have no hope today, Take away the hate from people, Lord and give them love, joy and peace. When God blesses, no man can take it away, so bless us all! **Psalm**

27:14 KJV Wait on the LORD: be of good courage, and he shall strengthen thine heart: wait, I say, on the LORD.

Day 31

Father God please, remember me today. I need your blessing. I am trying hard to serve you but I feel like I am failing. I need you to strengthen me and my family. I am counting on you to provide for us, Lord. Amen. **Joshua 24:15** KJV And if it seem evil unto you to serve the LORD, choose you this day whom ye will serve; whether the gods which your fathers served that were on the other side of the flood, or the gods of the Amorites, in whose land ye dwell: but as for me and my house, we will serve the LORD.

AB ASPECT Books

We invite you to view the complete
selection of titles we publish at:
www.ASPECTBooks.com

We encourage you to write us
with your thoughts about this,
or any other book we publish at:
info@ASPECTBooks.com

ASPECT Books' titles may be purchased in
bulk quantities for educational, fund-raising,
business, or promotional use.
bulksales@ASPECTBooks.com

Finally, if you are interested in seeing
your own book in print, please contact us at:
publishing@ASPECTBooks.com

We are happy to review your manuscript at no charge.